101 AWESOME
BUILDS

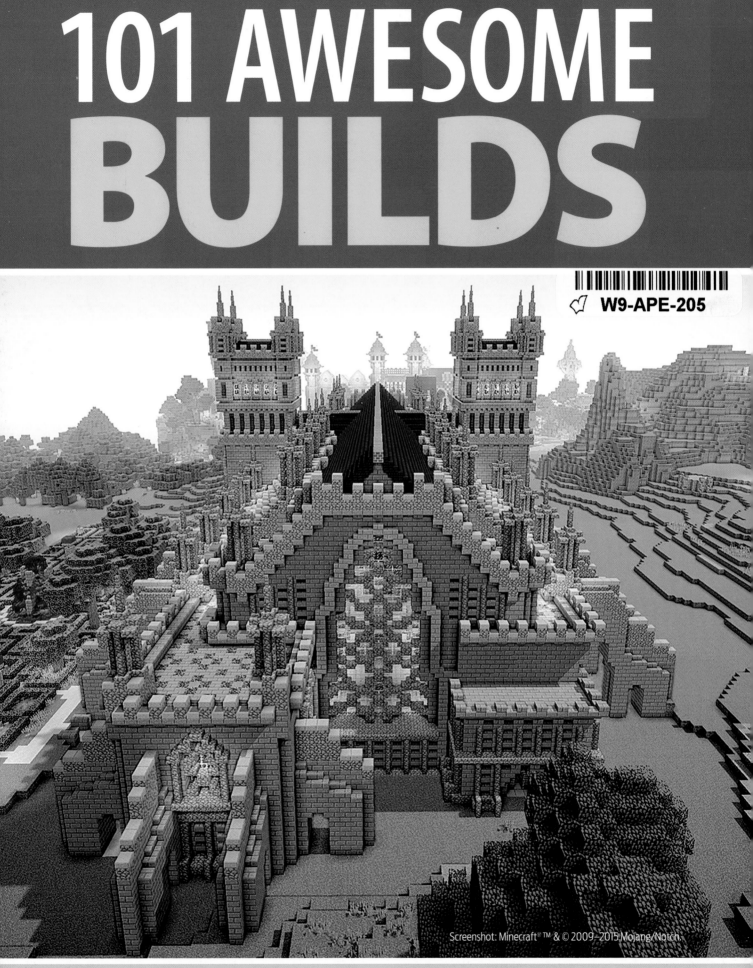

MINECRAFT® ™ SECRETS FROM THE WORLD'S GREATEST 'CRAFTERS

This book is available in quantity at special discounts for your group
or organization. For further information, contact:

Triumph Books LLC
814 North Franklin Street
Chicago, Illinois 60610
Phone: (312) 337-0747
www.triumphbooks.com

Printed in U.S.A.
ISBN: 978-1-62937-181-8

Content packaged by Mojo Media, Inc.
Joe Funk: Editor
Jason Hinman: Creative Director
Trevor Talley, Barry MacDonald, and Jackson Fast: Writers

CONTENTS

Introduction

Where would you live, if you could? Where would you travel to, if there were nothing holding you back? If you could create the most beautiful, amazing place or thing you can imagine, what would it look like?

Everyone has a unique answer: from fantastic castles striking against the sky of exotic lands with their tremendous towers, to glimmering spaceships in far-flung galaxies, we all have a place or thing living in our imaginations that we think would be the very best, if it could only exist.

This book is full of those places and things, those dream locations and creations that people keep

inside their head. Here, however, they have done the unthinkable and actually been brought to life through a type of magic. That, readers, is the magic of a video game called Minecraft.

Minecraft is really more than a game- it's a medium to convey what's inside your head. It's a gateway for imagination, a method to make dreams come to life that anyone can pick up, but which it takes true vision and patience to master.

Here, we've collected the realized dreams of the true masters of Minecraft that can take imagination and make it a real thing to see, explore and, in many cases, adore.

One hundred and one builds of the highest quality are what you'll find here, spanning every major category of creation that there is in this game. From science fiction to modernity to that crazed genius world of Redstone engineering; it's all here. And, that there are far more fantasy builds than any others is no coincidence: all builds herein have some of the fantastical about them, and some focus on it entirely, for fantasy is really another word for imagination, and Minecraft is imagination's game.

It's a journey that awaits you in these pages, a journey through many imaginations and the incredible things that lie waiting within them. You'll see castles, computers, musical instruments, deep dungeons, starships, and more, and all of them are shown off in the highest-resolution, most gorgeous images we could manage to capture.

We feel like we say it every year, and every year it's just as true as it was the last: this is the best time that Minecraft has ever had, the best time to get into the game, and the time when the best creations are being born. This book is a celebration of that time, and of the best that Minecraft has to offer.

Come with us through these 101 Minecraft builds, and step into the dreams of the world's best Minecraft creators, where anything is possible, and everything is made real, one block at a time.

Science Fiction

ASGARD HYBRID BATTLE CARRIER
By: Rossky

This absolutely massive spaceship is meant to be in the vanguard of an attack and bristles with weapons, but what's interesting is that it started out as a small support ship. As Crafter Rossky continued to work on it, it just kept getting bigger, and the end result is the behemoth you see here. This is an excellent example of how a project can evolve organically, and a good reason to just go with whatever creative impulses take you when building! The Asgard Hybrid Battle Carrier is 1,084 blocks long, 253 wide, and 116 tall for a total of 1,145,695 blocks, which took Rossky four weeks to build.

THE CHARITY
By: ImACow

There ain't much that's cooler than a futuristic sky city, and one with a full-on fantasy castle hanging from it? That's just about the coolest it gets. Built for a contest, ImACow and friends initially were going for an Arabic-inspired build, and then added on the idea of the future sky city to make it even cooler. The concept here is that Steve (the main character of Minecraft) decided to rescue the city of Arcadia by attaching a big ole space city to it and carrying it off into the sky (though he had to knock down most of the main tower to do so). The story goes quite a bit farther than that, and in fact you can actually read it in its entirety at the link for The Charity on Planet Minecraft. This extreme attention to detail goes even farther with this build, extending to the creators slaving over every facet of the inside and outside of the build, and they say that players should press every button they see in here, as they almost all perform some kind of cool effect. To give you an idea of how hard these guys worked on The Charity, ImACow says, "[I] even remembered my group and I spending 15 minutes debating between putting a birch or oak sapling on a pot in a secluded area." Now that's commitment!

CONXUNTO DE VENTO – THE HANGING CITY

By: Huggers

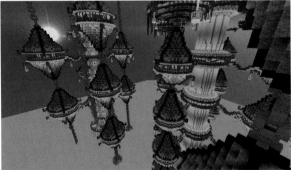

A fantastically inventive city from another time, or perhaps another planet, Conxunto features livable pods hung by chains from a large central spire. According to the builder Huggers, the 56 houses and 16 shops were left empty for players to fill up with their own decorations and items, and there is a Wheat farm and 9 parks for people to enjoy. Of particular note here in terms of building is the attention to detail on chains; Huggers even went so far as to include weights at the end of them, which while not needed in Minecraft (as there is no wind to move the blocks), lends a sense of reality to the whole build.

FUTURISTIC CITY
By: MCFRArchitect

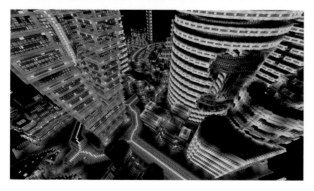

Recreating realistic-looking buildings is an impressive feat, but culling forth a new, fresh style of architecture and then implementing it on a huge scale is something else altogether. Throw in a complete concept like Futuristic City's five districts across as many islands, and you've got a build that truly stands out. The sweeping, cutout filled designs of these buildings are quite inventive, and the whole thing has a very organized and thought-through aesthetic that makes it a treat to explore. And with a city center, residential area, stadium, university, and even a spaceport, it'll be a while before you see all of this enormous build!

HYDROS
By: MicroMega

Some builds have such a giant scope and realized architecture that they actually can give you a bit of real-world vertigo. Hydros is one of these, as when you dive into the water from which its many complexes and buildings emerge, you really can get a sense of something huge looming just next to you. The idea of building something under water is nothing new in Minecraft, but rarely has it been completed on this scale or this creatively. Using a style that's part sci-fi, part Gothic-inspired, and even a little fantastical, builder MicroMega has created a lavishly detailed rendering of their idea of what the city of the future could look like, and even has gone so far as to add realistic details like an Opera house and a building dedicated to producing food for the whole city. The vistas on this one are really magnificent, and it even looks stunning at night, with all those buildings glowing in the water.

IRATION THE SUBMARINE CITY
By: loki0841

Initially built on the WoK server in the Beachtown area, Iration the Submarine City is meant to glide through the oceans. "Like a ghost under water, it's travelling silently in the oceans, hiding from the rest of the world." It's even built to be undetectable from both radar and sonar, and it is self-sustaining. Having this kind of a high concept when going into a build is a great idea, as it can really direct where the build goes. In this case, while the outside of Iration is all sleek and utilitarian, the inside is quite pleasing and feels like a cross between a cruise ship, a mall, and a fancy modern home. We think we'd be more than okay with living inside Iration!

SKY INN
By: CyRRaXxHD

Most of our steampunk stuff goes in the fantasy section, since the aesthetic and tech are more of an older design than the other builds here, but the neatly designed Sky Inn goes here primarily because of what (fictionally) powers it to float serenely above the waters that it travels across. Those would be the four quantum reactors that sit at the bottom of the Inn, which most certainly are some high-tech science fiction. Using some mods to get the sun and the waves looking more realistic, this build really does feel like a nice spot for weary travelers to rest on their journeys across the sea, and that the interiors are all done up as well is, as always, a very nice touch that gives the build depth and life. You can see the influence of the game that inspired this build, Bioshock Infinite, but it still manages to be something all its own through the personal touches put on by builder CyRRaXxHD.

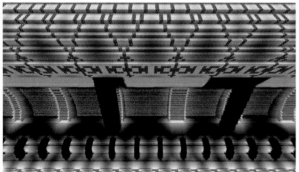

OCEAN FUTURE OF MANKIND
By: Waterijsje

Inspired by highly futuristic concepts of self-sustaining underwater/space cities, the Future of Mankind is a giant underwater hall filled with structures that represent resource collectors and water purifiers. It kind of has a Dune water collector/Halo ring city/Arthur C. Clake space capsule city thing going on, but with a very contemporary and bright design, using many beiges and warm colors on big, clean spaces to create a build that looks stunning when you use shaders to give it shadows and better lightning. Though there's not much to actually do in this build, it is very big (1,000 blocks long) and quite beautiful, and the construction is a bit more abstract than many of the other sci-fi builds in this book in a way that really works for it.

**OCEAN FUTURE
OF MANKIND**

P.I.E. PLANT INVESTIGATION EXPERIMENTS
By: CrashCraftPro (VigourBuilds)

P.I.E. isn't a building, it's a machine, and one with a story and a purpose. The P.I.E. is designed to travel the world and reside temporarily where there are rare plants, on which its massive frame does experiments in order to try and find a way to save the world. Alternatively, its crew of six technicians and scientists is trying to find a plant that can produce more oxygen to use in a space station, so that the people of Earth can leave their doomed planet. With the apocalypse still decades away, P.I.E. spends 10 years in each location before moving on to the next, and in the interim its precious cargo and expensive frame is protected by 15 mini helicopters from would-be raiders. Perhaps even more impressive than the thoroughly rich and unique concept for this build is that it was created by one single builder using no outside software, something rare for a build of this size and detail.

TEWERAN SURVIVAL GAMES 3

By: Rubikapulla, Mickare, LueckeFelix, Scorchy91, Kellerbier, Kime8, DJpaulii, RRMonty, Carp_13, Assikuh, _Tenku_, WizardBlockHD

Teweran is a map found on the Hive server, one of the more popular Minecraft servers online, and it's probably both the best Survival Games-style map and the best future city we've ever seen in the game. For those unfamiliar, the Survival Games is a mode of play that essentially recreates the rules from *The Hunger Games* movies and books in Minecraft, with a group of players starting in the city with no items or weapons and having to then battle each other until just one is left. Teweran is insanely detailed, full of secret Chests and all manner of buildings and decorations. Unlike most city builds, it even goes so far as to realistically include a small "countryside" of plains and landscapes, giving it a very complete and believable feel.

Fantasy and Ancient

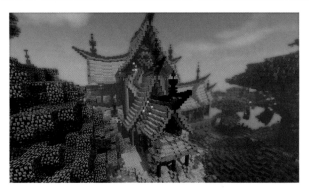

A THAI THEMED JUNGLE MAP

By: Whisper974

Maybe this is from a mythical eastern-inspired world, or maybe it's an ancient temple in Thailand itself, but either way there's something quite magical about this build that sits serenely in the deep jungle. Builder Whisper974 says that this creation was inspired by eating in a Thai restaurant, which just tells you that inspiration for something great is everywhere! The curves on the roof here are particularly nice, as is the fact that a nice stone base was created for the whole thing to sit on. We also love the trees, under which you can find all sorts of nice details like little extra huts. For being such a calm, peaceful looking place, it might surprise you that this map was actually made to be used for PvP, but on second look we can totally see a battle ragin' across this beautiful structure and the land it sits on.

AANDOVALE GROVE

By: Aandolaf

Nature in a giant valley with a large structure was the thought behind Aandovale Grove, which features magnificent columned structures covered in greenery commanding said valley, which is lush itself. There are some really lovely architectural elements in this, which sorta take Greek architectural elements from the ancient past and amplify them into something fantastical with a bit of a Rivendell/Minas Tirith *Lord of the Rings* thing goin' on, too. The hanging homes and lanterns in the towering trees are nice touches, and they, along with the rest of the build, are a must-see at night as well.

AQUOSIA TEMPLE OF THE WATER GOD
By: mkisner328

The full beauty of this already gorgeous floating temple build is only revealed if you know the secret, but don't worry, we'll let you in on it. All you gotta do is hang out between the angels at the top of the Temple and wait for night to fall, and then Water will flow from the angels and through the air in a beautiful spiral, something that would seem impossible even in Minecraft. The trick to this impressive build is that there are "invisible blocks" that hold up the Water, something that not many builds incorporate because they take a lot of work. The Water is activated with Daylight Sensors that release it when the sun goes down. Crazy as that is, the angel part of the Temple is just part of this build that soars into the sky, so if you check it out, make sure to peep below the angels as well so you get the full effect.

AVARICIA

By: Schnogot

Good jumpin' jackrabbits this is a pretty build. The cohesiveness and balance of the overall design is astounding to begin with, but it's in the decorative details like the many arches, buttresses, the texturing on the walls, and the use of the green as a secondary color bring this build from great to stupendous. If that weren't enough, the innards of this city are just as painstakingly crafted, as is the "wild beach" and the island-dotted lake that it features. Even cooler, it's set up to be a PvP map with a secret treasure, with the idea being that 24 people take each other on in this map while seeking treasure and weapons. Only one can leave, and as Schnogot asks on Planet Minecraft, "Will it be you?"

BERYL LOCH
By: QuikFox

Most forts and castles in Minecraft are of the epic, sweeping fantasy style, similar to the Disney castle or those of famous TV shows and movies. In real life, there are all manner of forts and castles, and the architecture of each depends on the time period it was built in and the people who built it. Many forts around the dark ages were much smaller and more compact than those we typically see in Minecraft, being built with scant resources and labor and being entirely for defense, not looks. That's the case for Beryl Loch, about which creator QuikFox says, "I wanted to make this fort very simple and square as the lore for it places it very early in the history of the world. It would be one of the very first castles built and as such it wouldn't be too decorative or effective right away." There is a large amount of story to this build, in fact, the whole of which involves a paranoid emperor and can be found at the Planet Minecraft page.

THE CARMINE BODEGA ON THE ALABASTER COAST

By: QuikFox

QuikFox is just so good at building ancient-inspired fantasy structures that there are rich, deeply thought-out backstories for each excellent structure. Here's an excerpt from the Planet Minecraft page on The Carmine Bodega: "The Alabaster Coast is best known for the Carmine Bodega perched upon its seaside cliffs, known far and wide for its beautiful architecture. This specific region has never been officially named as it is, technically, part of the Stonehollow Vale, however it has become known as the Alabaster Coast because of the brilliant white of its seaside cliffs. The Carmine Bodega is, in essence, a huge market with almost no permanent residents. It is, effectively split into three different areas, the Inner Market for specialty and luxury goods, the Outer Market for mid-range goods, and the Lower Outer Market for common goods and supplies. Traders and merchants gather here to sell their wares and goods to each other. The market is so massive in importance that anything a person could desire is either found here or could be contracted to be obtained; nothing is seemingly unavailable."

CASTLE HILL
By: Aandolaf

If QuikFox is all about the more realistic-looking, if still fantastical, builds, Aandolaf has made a name for their giant structures that run closer to the fantasy stereotype, though they're still just as impressively detailed and even beautiful. In fact, Aandolaf says that the inspiration for this castle came partly from the castle that inspired that of Sleeping Beauty, known as the Neuschwanstein Castle. Inspiration was also drawn from the Butrón Castle, a real Spanish castle originally built in the Middle Ages, but restructured in the late 1800s to its now iconic look.

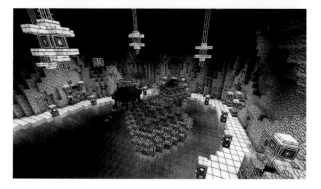

THE CAVERN OF NAKETH
By: Turbo_Cass

Underground cities and structures are quite popular subjects for creations in Minecraft, which makes a lot of sense considering that the game naturally spawns caves into the world that make for great building locations. Some people, however, take things to the extreme by creating some truly epic underground sprawls like The Cavern of NaKeth. The story for this build, and there is a pretty complex one, is that Steve found the Cavern on his explorations and began documenting the "elf-like beings, who call themselves Ateryians" he found there. The massive trees in this cave are worshipped by the Ateryians, and the biggest of all, NaKeth, is their main deity and the namesake of the Cavern itself. Certainly one of the best realized cave builds, and a really fun one to explore.

CASTELLUM ROMANORUM
By: edsinger

Server hubs come in all shapes, sizes, and even time periods, this one being a sort of ancient Roman/fantasy castle-inspired build. It's a very big hub, and one that could house a lot of portals to different parts of a server, and it has a very mature look to it that many hubs don't. The domes and the textured walls are particularly nice, and there's some very cool detailing in the water with some underwater columns.

CLOUDHAVEN
By: lynchyinc

Cityships are another genre of building that you'll see here and there on Minecraft sites, as is steampunk (something you'll see all the time), but CloudHaven is almost definitely the most jam-packed ship we've ever seen that still looks like it was professionally designed. It almost looks like a creature, like some sort of fish robot swimming through the sky, but in the "reality" of the build it's an old mining ship that, after a catastrophe known as the "Void Storm" took away all of the land in the world, CloudHaven was converted to a cityship with other 1,000 "traders, skylords, merchants, smugglers, pirates and proletariat alike" living on it. There is a cool set of challenges associated with this map, mostly based around trying to survive and finding things in the ship like the treasury room, which is a cool twist on the standard steampunk sky map.

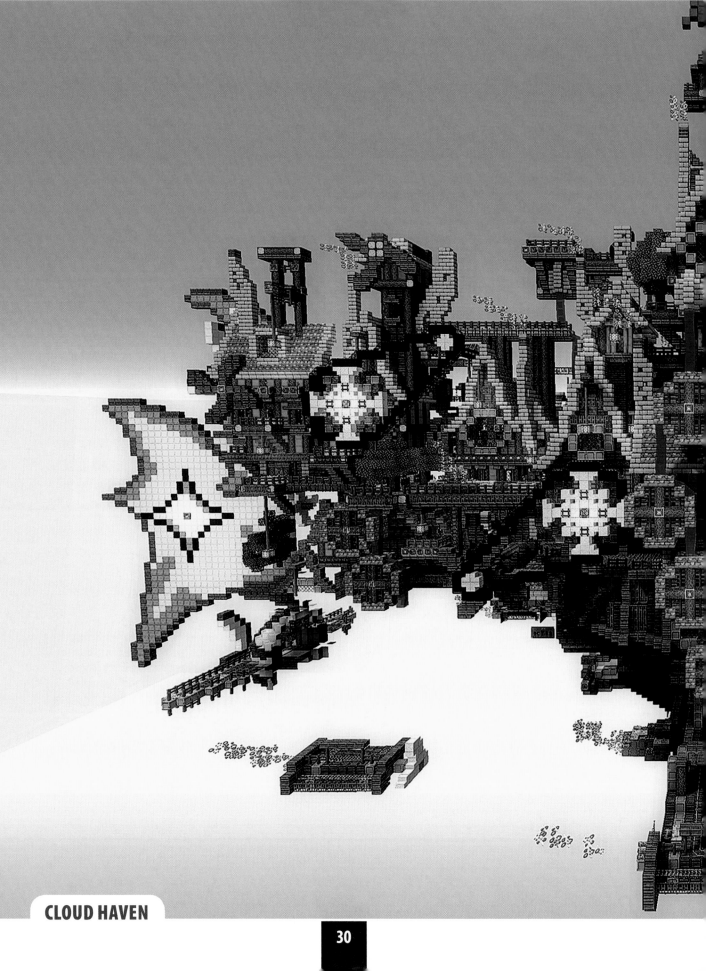

CLOUD HAVEN

COURTMERE PALACE
By: DJpaulii

From the famous and popular Teweran server, this magnificent and massive palace with a Neo-Gothic architecture style is heavily based on a real-world building called the Rathaus, which is the City Hall of Vienna in Austria. This one, though, is a looooot bigger than the Rathaus, taking 270,000 blocks to build, and it features a huge number of real-world architectural features like buttresses, arches, towers, and more. This is one of those that you could actually use to study in an architecture class, and it makes you wonder if DJpaulii took any such classes; it's just that good.

DESERT CITY OF ALKAZARA!

By: Jeracraft

A stupendous green-domed palace towers over this city, known as Alkazara, but there's so much more to see in this city than just the admittedly excellent palace. Wander the streets and you'll find a city that almost seems to live and breathe, including everything from homes to farms to docks to towers. It's really a beautifully realized urbanscape, and one that feels like it was created to scale from a real world ancient city.

DREADFORT PALACE PIRATE FORT

By: jefe070

The "residence of the Pirate Lord of the Iron Shore," this is a mighty, commanding wooden castle that sits alone atop the ocean, waiting for the ships of its pirate fleet to return with plunder and tales of conquest. It has, according to PMC, 100 cannons to defend it and four "illegally obtained" heavy bombardment cannons, meaning nothing gets through to it to even begin to threaten the Dreadfort. It also has a small fleet of ships all its own, which are themselves nicely designed, and all of this build has a great dangerous-looking aesthetic due to the use of a lot of black and brown.

ELBANE'S ARRIVAL
By: MrD4nny

The very first time we loaded up Elbane's Arrival, we didn't really know how big the dragon (the one the name Elbane belongs to) in it would be, or where it would be. When we turned around and had this huge thing loading up right behind us, all fangs and glowing eyes, it actually put fear into us. Feeling something that big right behind you, even virtually, is pretty dang freaky. That should tell you all you need to know to want to check this build out, but there's more to it as well. Elbane is attacking a city called Desnig on a floating air island, which is well designed itself and lends an excellent sense of drama to the build.

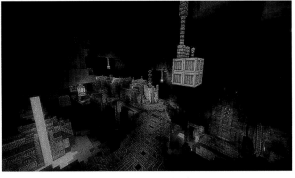

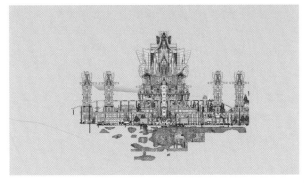

THE ETERNAL FORTRESS OF NAR
By: carloooo

One heck of a builder, carloooo is one of our most loved creators in Minecraft, because he always goes way above and beyond no matter the build to do something quite special. For instance, this build was meant to be a simple spawn build for a server, but carloooo went a bit nuts and churned out one of the coolest, most hardcore forts we've ever seen. As he says (and is quite proud of), it even has MOVABLE CANNONS! So cool. This is one of those that is best experienced as you walk about it, crossing the expansive bridges that lead across the ditch to the fortress proper. There you will get nothing but the best in exterior and interior work that a creative and driven mind like carloooo's will produce, not to mention excessive attention paid to the grounds of the build as well.

FERRODWYNN TOWNCENTER
By: mega_franco

There's a trend on sites like Planet Minecraft for people who have big, popular builds, especially those on servers, to lift small parts of their larger builds and upload them for others to explore. That's what happened with the Ferrodwynn Towncenter, which is part of a muuuch, much larger Ferrodwynn town from the FRealms.tk server. It's great on its own or as a hub, with its convenient wheel shape, and it contains (according to PMC): "The circular Old Town with a small church and lots of small houses and streets, 4 gates and 4 different styled bridges, the moat, 24 unique huge and noble houses (no copy and paste, a pirate house ;), and a lovely detailed tavern."

FORBIDDEN CITY
By: bohtauri

In the flesh 'n blood world, the Forbidden City is the famous (and infamous) palace in China that was the home of the emperor from 1420 to 1912, an insane stretch of time for any place to remain a capital. It is enormous in real life (it still exists in much the same condition as it did for centuries, with 980 buildings over 180 acres). In what is almost shocking for its impressiveness, bohtauri has recreated this massive complex in a 1:1 ratio in this build, with every building represented.

HANGING GARDENS OF AZYROS
By: Pikipikipuku

Another build with a historical counterpart, this one isn't a 1:1 or even a full recreation of a real place (this one doesn't exist anymore), but these hanging gardens are based on the once-existing Hanging Gardens of Babylon that were one of the Seven Wonders of the Ancient World. This build took Pikipikipuku four months and is a beautiful mosaic of stone, color and plants, and it's so big that it took our machine over 20 minutes just to render what you see in the photos here.

JM GOTHIC HOUSE
By: JamziboyMinecraft

Big builds are super cool, but many of those stunning sprawlers of builds are made up of a bunch of smaller builds like houses and other buildings, and making those good is just as important to the overall build as the giant palaces are. That's the thought behind JM's Gothic House here, along with many other such smaller builds. It's nice sometimes to recognize excellence in these littler builds, we believe, and the old-world architecture of this particular creation is top-notch in our book.

KELESTRIA
By: MrPorteEnBois

Builders often join teams in order to get more exposure for their works and to collaborate on big builds, and that's where this build came from. MrPorteEnBois is part of the Neolesia team and concocted this honker of a castle for them. The blue and white combo is striking and gives it a very particular look, and if you'll notice, this thing is almost as tall as the very large mountain just behind the castle itself. This one is all about exterior, not having an interior, but for that it's one of the nicer large castles out there, with detailing to the extreme.

KELESTRIA

MEDIEVAL BUILD CONTEST WORLD
By: BebopVox

As you might be able to tell from this chapter, the impetus to build a medieval town is one that many people share. What you might not be able to tell from the high quality of medieval and fantasy builds here is that the huge number of fantasy and medieval builds out there means that there are a lot of them that really aren't that impressive. It takes a lot of thought and some actual research to make a build stand out in a genre that's enormously popular. BebopVox knows this, and you can see the research that went into this world. There's a whole functioning town's worth of buildings here, from the keep to the houses to the graveyard and the gallows that, if this were a real world city, would presumably be where the graveyard gets its contents. BebopVox has done the medieval thing right by this build, and the result is that anyone wandering this town can absolutely feel like they are living in the feudal ages.

ROMECRAFT COLOSSEUM
By: stugace

A perfect ellipse built with cubes? Yep, that's the Romecraft Colosseum, a build that was meant to be as close to a real life colosseum as possible, and which draws heavy influence from the Colosseum in Rome. This build is 189x156x48 blocks and has 456 outer support columns. The builders were so concerned with being accurate to ancient Roman structures that they take the time on their Planet Minecraft page to point out that, while the Rome Colosseum had pillars 4m thick, this build was forced to make theirs 3m thick due to not being able to make round shapes in Minecraft. Regardless, it is a remarkably accurate representation of an ancient, famous structure, and it looks quite striking with shaders on.

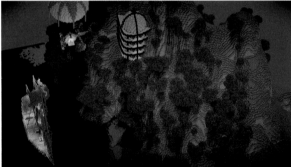

RYU SAKAI THE DRAGON REALM
By: AAmdahl

Balloons, dragons, ships and sea: that's what the Ryu Sakai build is all about. As per the Planet Minecraft page, this build has: "6 floating islands, 4 airships, 2 dragons + 1 phoenix + 1 sea serpent, and much much more for you to explore :D." Like many builds in this book, this one comes from a big-time server originally, that being the Team Vareide server. There's a heavy Asian influence in this build that combines things like Chinese-style dragons and Japanese cherry blossom trees with more western-design ships and some kinda sci-fi/Asian buildings to great effect. It'd be a neat world to live in, if a bit scary with all those massive dragons hanging about, that's for sure!

SAILOR'S HIDEOUT
By: Shady og Ola

We just can't say enough for a good, small build put in just the right place and done just the right way. Sailor's Hideout, with its frame that would be diminutive in a regular Minecraft landscape but which stands out tremendously against the flat ocean setting on which it exists, is one such build. Its creator calls it a "relaxed build" and invites the player to "settle down and enjoy the environment," and when you combine that sentiment with its telling name, you can really get a feel for the mood of this build. It's a place for hard-working sailors who have braved the dangers of the deep to come and take some time off, maybe because they need to get out from under the eye of some lawful force or another for a bit, and the build gets that feeling perfectly right.

SATINE'S PALACE
By: Antiqua

"In the age of Emperors and magick, there lived a woman of no particular beauty. She was plain, with sharp curves, dark flowing hair, and tanned skin from working in the fields. Her name was Satine." So begins the tale on the Planet Minecraft page for this build, which goes on to lay out a story of a magical girl blessed by Mother Earth who sacrificed herself to save her land from starving and from the evil wizard who caused the blight that led to such a calamity. As a reward for her service to the land, the Emperor had built a palace/tomb for the dying Satine, who had spent her last strength saving everyone, and that is this build. Outside of its heart-wrenching story, this build is just neatly done, with an entrance that rivals just about any other, and a cool concept that involves placing an underwater palace in the center of a ring of impassable mountains.

SHARTHUR

By: RoloFolo

Many Minecraft builds that become popular are works in progress, and it can be really fun and rewarding to follow a build as its creators complete work on it over a long period of time. Though Sharthur is no longer being updated, it was once this kind of build, and the quality that you now see in this build that excels at the medieval thing is a result of that process. When you see a really excellent build, just remember that even if you feel your skills could never be at the level of the build you see, the people who created it almost always took a great deal of time to refine that build into the seemingly perfect thing that you now see, and that they all were at your own skill level at one point. Practice and persistence are the name of the game in Minecraft, as they are in most skill-based endeavors.

S'KORN DRAKAS
By: Darth_waffle

We'd like to just take a moment before we dive into this build to focus on the fact that its creator probably has the greatest handle in all of gaming, that being the incredibly poignant Darth_waffle. Moving beyond that undeniable fact, S'korn Drakas is our only Lava build, because frankly people just don't build on Lava that much. This, however, is one of the best builds in the entire book both for its original setting and the fact that it just really pulls it off its aesthetic, that being a 300k+ block dark elf fortress built to stave off the attacks of a "giant dragon" set on "cutting a swathe of destruction from East to West." We like that it eschews the stereotypical castle/fortress look for something more Byzantine, and we think it looks just great framed by all that glowing Lava.

STEAMPUNK CITY
By: the Gravi'team

If CloudHaven is the steampunk cityship to end all such ships, the Gravi'team's Steampunk City may well be the steampunk city to do the same. The wide-out view of this build tells the most about it, with its tremendous water wheel that you can just hear groaning in your imagination providing the most obvious focal point for what is a truly busy build, but one which is so in a way that makes it feel complete and not over-stuffed at all. The island setting lends it a bit of the steam pirate vibe as well, and imagining an anime or graphic novel set in this awesome city is not hard to do at all.

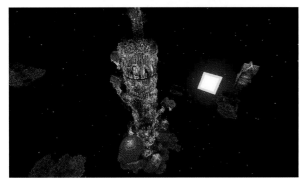

STORTIC'S SKYHOUSE
By: TheCraftMiner

TheCraftMiner (another great name) is the builder for this odd tower, which is a bit of a steampunk/natural build/tower mash-up. This is a contest build, originally made for Planet Minecraft's Minecraft Sky Limit Project Contest, which saw a number of excellent entries. The inventiveness is strong with this one, that takes the concept of a tall structure and layers it with a ton of variety, including a lot of plant life and some great little cottages and houses hanging around the main structure. It's no wonder this one went far in a contest, and we commend TheCraftMiner for executing their vision here.

THIEVES' FORT
By: mackmo

Also known as Forest Manor, the Thieves' Fort is a lesson in the idea that fantasy doesn't necessarily have to look completely out of this world, but can instead resemble something very realistic. It is, as mackmo calls it, a "castle/mansion thingy," but it's so much more than that in terms of design, looking quite like a Gothic structure that could easily exist in the forests of Europe, complete with a giant clock tower that looks out over the whole thing and breaks up the view nicely. This is one where the location that was obviously crafted just for the build is very important, and you can almost hear the howl of the wolves in the surrounding forest in your head as you gaze at this castle after night has fallen in the game.

TEMPLE OF AREATHEOX

By: YanniickZ

Floatin' temples are good stuff, and the Temple of Areatheox by YanniickZ puts most others to shame, even in this automatically cool category. Though YanniickZ claims to be bad at storytelling, this particular build has a really interesting concept, which is that it is the literal heaven for the people that live in the nearby village. Anyone who dies there is reborn here, not all that far away, and as a heavenly setting, we think the villagers could do much worse. The spikiness here is a nice touch, giving it the feel of something created from a very specific and oldschool fantasy culture, perhaps maybe even being something built by elves. Whoever the original designers (in this fantasy world), they did a darn good job, as did YanniickZ.

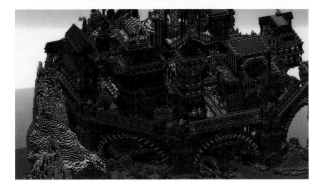

VORPAL CITY
By: salmon77

Vorpal City has a lot goin' on, something you can tell right off from the text that accompanies its post on Planet Minecraft: "Vorpal City! Nestled on a grand delta sits this magnificent site...Truly a wonder to behold! A fully detailed build, from every nook and cranny of the exterior and interiors touched. This Steampunk Victorian city was founded upon the ideals of progress, as well as the gap between rich and poor, and a how a government may manipulate both these castes. Vorpal City is split into two halves...Impossible you say? Why we believe if you can cut a simple sandvich in half you can certainly cut a city right down the middle, making a lower, and upper city!" That certainty becomes even more certain when you look at this beauty, where salmon77 and friends have made it a virtual reality, splitting it neatly in the center.

VITRUVIAN CASTLE

By: RezolutnyDarek

RezolutnyDarek makes builds often inspired by real-life structures, and this one falls within that paradigm, being based mostly on the Castle Peles of Romania. It's part of a much larger build, as many in this book are, being the primary castle for RezolutnyDarek's Vitruvian City, a great build in its own right. It has everything a good castle from the period when looks were more important than defense should, including towers, courtyards and dozens of windows overlooking the beautiful countryside that surrounds this lovely castle. The spires and spikes atop the buildings are just a few of many creative touches that amplify this build from cool to spectacular, and all of RezolutnyDarek's builds have the same attention to detail that this exemplifies.

WATER TEMPLE
By: RedJohnxS

Using Stone Bricks almost exclusively to create a cool build is very hard to do, but through the creation of a structure that is at once modular and organic-feeling, Water Temple entirely pulls off this difficult concept. We've spent a lot of time wandering on Minecraft servers, and this build feels just like the kind of thing that has taken our breath away when we stumbled across it after hours of seeing the same plain vanilla Minecraft landscape go by. Builder RedJohnxS says that they were watching *Lord of the Rings* and trying to fill up an entire island with the most complex structure they could, and that sounds like as good of a way to get inspired to a great build as any that we've heard of.

Modern

AIRPORT
By: mextremel

There's nothing wrong with castles and spaceships and all that fantastical stuff, but there's something truly impressive when a person can recreate something from real life in Minecraft and actually make it feel like the real deal. Even more so when it's not just a shell of a build or one that vaguely represents the real thing, but is a build that proves that the creator obviously studied the subject and attempted to recreate it in a way that makes it feel like it lives and breathes. That, Crafters, is why this Airport is so awesome. It doesn't just have buildings and planes, it has detailed representations of real life planes down to small features, and even goes so far as to have everything from airport bars and ticket counters and security checkpoints to the fuel tankers, fire-brigade vehicles, and baggage trains that you'd find at a real world airport.

BEACH TOWN MALL
By: Kielbasa

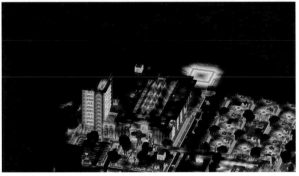

Part of a much bigger build called Beach Town, the Beach Town Mall is a full-fledged modern shopping experience in Minecraft. Walking about this build, you can almost imagine the smell of Cinnabons and the gentle murmur of hundreds of shoppers' voices, and you might even start to wonder which entrance you parked at. It's a great example of an idea that is far outside of the stereotypical castles and ships box that Minecrafters often find themselves thinking in while also being something that everyone is already familiar with and could probably build their own version of. Why not give it a try yourself?

DUNYAZADE OASIS HOME

By: Tech Zero

In the deep desert, your home needs every bit of shelter it can get from the unrelenting sun. That's the concept behind the most brilliant feature of the all-around excellent Dunyazade Oasis Home, which has the only sun shade sails we've ever seen on Minecraft build. The house itself is design perfection as well, incorporating both modern and traditional desert architecture seamlessly. This is a fully decked out home, including multiple sleeping spaces and quite a few idyllic chill-out areas, where Crafters can watch the sun set from the safety of the shade.

CONTEMPORARY MUSEUM
By: Joueur_inconnu

This is one of our favorite builds by one of our favorite builders. It pulls off the fascinating trick of looking almost exactly like its real-life counterparts (that being modern museums), which in Minecraft's blocky world is quite hard to do. It's also a great mash-up of modern and ancient architecture in a way that absolutely makes sense, as well as a tremendous lesson in architecture and compound design. The creator uses water perfectly, and each building is laid out to specific dimensions. We wouldn't be surprised to hear that Joueur_inconnu is a real-life architect or has some training in the field, and this kind of build shows that Minecraft can be used as a tool for training in such fields as design and architecture. Really though, who could say blocky buildings and straight lines are boring after looking at this? An absolutely beautiful build.

**CONTEMPORARY
MUSEUM**

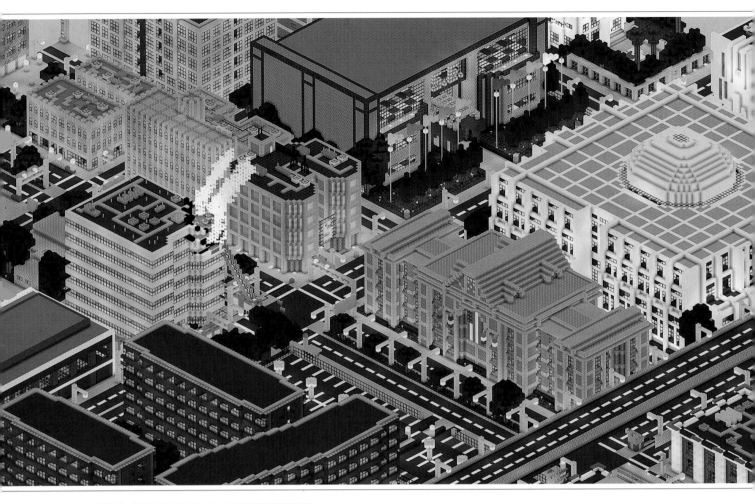

GREENFIELD
By: THEJESTR, KristofferAndre, TrippleX, and team

Every build in this chapter is remarkable for its recreation of something real (or that could be), but only one build claims to be the "most realistic modern city in Minecraft," and that's the city of Greenfield. This is one of the most famous builds in Minecraft, with over 1 million total views on Planet Minecraft, and it is just huge. It has been under construction for years, and it includes just about every kind of neighborhood, district and feature of a city you can think of. There are towering skyscrapers, sprawling suburbs, ruins and areas under construction, docks, factories, shops, and literally everything a city could have. Every Crafter should give this one a good, hard exploration.

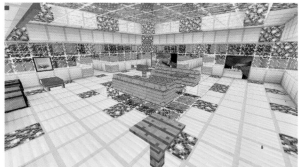

HOUSE IN THE WATER
By: Darkscour

Building a home in Minecraft entirely under water is harder than you'd think, though many good builders have pulled it off. While this might not be the biggest one, it is probably the most realistic, resembling scientific installations that are used by marine biologists and other researchers to stay underwater all the time. That's why, while this is not really a recreation of a real life thing, we've put it in the modern category, because it really is not that different from the underwater living places that exist, nor is it impossible to imagine something almost exactly like this being common in the near future. We love the modular nature of the build, and especially like the addition of the viewing tower jutting out of the water, where the undersea dwellers can come up for some air without having to leave the home.

OASIS OF THE SEAS TERMINAL 18

By: CharlesGoldburn

CharlesGoldburn is almost unquestionably Minecraft's premier cruise boat builder. Among his many, many boats he has painstakingly recreated in Minecraft in a 1:1 scale (meaning they are as big in Minecraft as they are in real life) is the Oasis of the Seas boat, in this build seen at a docking terminal. Goldburn's boats are all recreations of real boats, and what makes them special versus the many, many other cruise boat recreations out there is that he goes above and beyond to detail these boats realistically. Just check out that above shot: you can see everything from deck chairs to bars to realistic railing! These ships are fully complete from the inside out, meaning there is virtual space for all of the 6,300 passengers and 2,394 crew in the 16 decks of the Oasis, a ship that is classified as the largest class of cruise ship in the world.

MATTUPOLIS
By: mattuFIN, Flowtogo

Another enormous modern city build, Mattupolis creator mattuFIN says of his work in progress: "Once complete, the city will consist of a diverse range of commercial, residential and industrial districts. [. . .]The city and its surroundings are mostly based on those of Vancouver, BC and Seattle, WA, but the architecture is also influenced by European cities such like Stockholm, Sweden."That description tells you everything you need to know about the level of research and knowledge of cities that went into Mattupolis. Malls, parks, a university, a dam, and 90+ skyscrapers are just a small number of the buildings in this incredible, dense build that is up there with the other major Minecraft cities in terms of complexity and pure awesomeness.

THE HUNT
By: BjornToBeWild

The exceptionally-named BjornToBeWild starts his Planet Minecraft profile off by saying, "Hey look, buddy. I'm a builder — that means I build things." One of those many things that the quite funny Bjorn has built is this mammoth of a mansion, which is meant to be a PvP map. While that would qualify it for our Competitions chapter, we like it here because what we really find tremendous about this build is its uncanny representation of a real-world manor home, including its crown jewel: a beautifully constructed geometric garden. Whether you enjoy this for its excellent aesthetics or want to take on your friends on its verdant grounds, The Hunt is a map to download for sure.

THE HUNT

MODERN MANSION

By: skoo

The Modern Mansion, created by skoo, is just a solid, great looking house with a balanced modern feel. The windows are especially well-incorporated, as is the entrance pool. Probably the coolest thing, to us, is that it uses tree leaves to create a very unique and creative fence that is quite similar to some topiary you'll see at such houses in the real world.

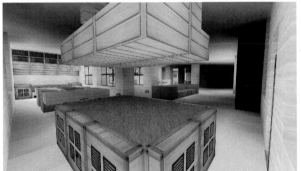

ITALIAN VILLA
By: RaptorAnka

RaptorAnka is a builder of modern homes and buildings in Minecraft, and this particular gem comes from the famed World of Keralis server (www.keralis.net). It sits neatly on a cliff in a neighborhood of similar homes, much like a true Italian villa might, and in addition to its lovely red-tile recreation exterior, its strength lies in the completeness of its interior design. Everything feels just like a real (and real expensive) home might, including expertly placed plants, sunken lighting and even a nearby vineyard! Quite the home indeed, from a master of the medium.

ITALIAN VILLA

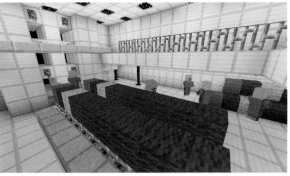

SOVIET SSGN-941 TYPHOON NUCLEAR SUBMARINE
By: Kanovalov

If boats and underwater houses are awesome, submarines have to be some freakish level of awesome that meshes together all that's good about the other two, plus torpedoes! This is a highly accurate recreation of a real world Soviet sub, and you can walk all the way through it seeing everything from those dangerous torpedo bays to the nuclear engines and all of the many crew rooms. In Russian, the name for this map is "Tsel' unichtozhena!" which means, "Target eliminated!" With the firepower that this beast commands, it's a phrase that you can easily imagine echoing off its metal walls when you walk through the SSGN-941.

NV
By: pigonge

A massively prolific house builder and creator in general, pigonge is a home creation master, and this is one of the builder's masterpieces. Not only does pigonge include incredible balance and sophisticated architecture in every build, especially giving focus to the use of various types of blocks to create different textures, pigonge is also as notable for amazing attention to the grounds. NV includes the standard pool, which is nothing new in housing builds, but does it in a fresh and attractive way. The tennis court though, is something you just don't see often, and that kind of overall excellence in the house-creation department is why pigonge truly can be called a master builder.

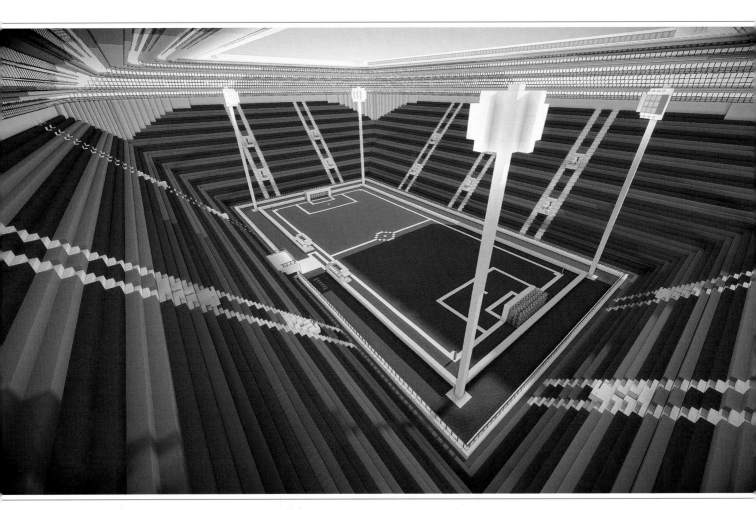

STADIUM

By: Roux

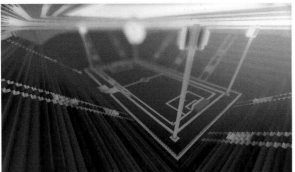

A stadium is a great idea for a build: it's symmetrical, it's big, everyone is familiar with them, and building one will help a player learn a lot of the basic rules of megabuilds without having to do something too difficult. That being said, this Stadium by Roux is a true standout build. It not only includes the seating and the outer structure, it actually has the entrance tunnels, the lighting, the goals, and even the stripes! That's commitment to an idea, and the execution is lacking in nothing.

VILLA MALDIVA
By: pigonge

Yep, another pigogne house makes it in, and that's because these things are just all around great examples of construction and concept. This one is more of a nature-including build than the other, with pigonge beautifully introducing greenery and landscaping to a barren desert land. And of course, there's another tennis court, because why wouldn't there be? This build serves as an excellent lesson in the idea that the land your build is on is just as important to making a build great as anything else.

Pop Culture

GALLIFREY CITADEL
By: themixedt4pe

Whovians will know what this one is, but for those who don't watch *Doctor Who*, this enclosed castle is located on the planet Gallifrey, which is where the highly powerful Time Lords (the good Doctor himself is one such being) originated. This is the Capitol of the Time Lords, also known as Gallifrey Citadel, and here it is rendered in what is pretty close to actual scale. This thing can be climbed from the inside, but we think it's best viewed as you fly about it.

ARENDELLE CASTLE
By: ilikecutepeople

Anyone who has seen a movie recently (or has ears) knows this build, even if they don't recognize it at first. This is the Arendelle Castle, famous for being one of the primary locations of the ridiculously popular movie *Frozen*. Once again we have to point out that this thing goes above and beyond by including not just the castle itself, but all of the surrounding land, and there are even some pretty cool little extra bits in this one like ships and some builds up in the (very nicely built) hills. Going even more above and beyond, there are actually two versions of this build, one in the summer and one, appropriately, in the winter. This is one we won't (WAIT FOR IT) be "letting go" of for a while!

ARENDELLE
CASTLE

FRANKLIN'S PAD
By: themixedt4pe

Grand Theft Auto V is one of the most successful open-world games ever; and of the many thousands of locations in that insanely huge game, Franklin's Pad is the one that almost all players of the game will recognize. You probably can't re-create the activities that Franklin himself does in said pad, but that doesn't mean you can't make it your own base from which to get up to whatever the Minecraft version of stealing digital cars is. Stealing your friend's Horse, maybe?

INFAMOUS
By: The NewHeaven team

The video game *Infamous* is the inspiration for this, one of the most colorful and creative city builds we've ever seen in the game. There is much to see in this extensive build, and what makes it special versus other city builds (besides the extremely high skill of the builders themselves, which is obvious from the moment you step into this creation) is that the fantastical world of the video game that it comes from allows its builders to pull from the best parts of reality and imagination to create something that is better than both. It's truly excellent, with surprises quite literally around every corner, and it is one of those builds that has hours worth of exploration contained within its wide bounds.

INFAMOUS

MINAS TIRITH
By: EpicQuestz

Ah, Minas Tirith! City of Gondor, in front of and verily inside of whose white walls the battle for the saving or destruction of Middle Earth was fought. Now, there are a whole buncha Minas Tiriths made in Minecraft- it just fits the aesthetic of the game so easily and has an iconic shape while leaving room for experimentation. That there is a lot of crossover between *Lord of the Rings* fans and Minecraft players is not much of a surprise- but by far the most popular version of Minas Tirith online is that by EpicQuestz. This build has over 280,000 views on Planet Minecraft, and for good reason: Epic has really gone above and beyond to both recreate what you see in the LOTR films and to add creative touches to its smaller buildings. It is, in all, a very pretty build that will take your breath away when you see it with shaders at sunset, and it takes quite a long time to explore all of its many houses, towers, and its book-and-film accurate seven layers. There are even dungeons and sewers!

USS EXCELSIOR, USS ENTERPRISE & USS RELIANT

By: Mozzie

This build is straight-up killer. It faithfully recreates the ships from *Star Trek* and their construction bays (though not at scale), and is actually walkable inside, which most Trek builds aren't. Throw some shaders on it and, as you can see, this build outright shimmers with high-tech pop culture beauty, making the iconic ship designs truly pop by using just the right materials. Do yourself a favor and beam into this one, especially if you're one of those who is looking for that final frontier of Minecraftery.

Competitions, Games, and Adventuring

BLOCKRIDER
By: Brutec

Minigames are pretty hard to make in Minecraft even when they don't get as complex as this one, but what Brutec here has done with this car-based minigame is a true feat. Using Minecarts, a whole bunch of Redstone, and some Command Blocks, BlockRider creates a game where you basically dodge cars as you fly down a road. It even tracks your points, and the traffic is randomly generated so each time you play is a new experience. Fly around this one a bit when you are done playing, as it's pretty cool to see the car storage and underlying Redstone.

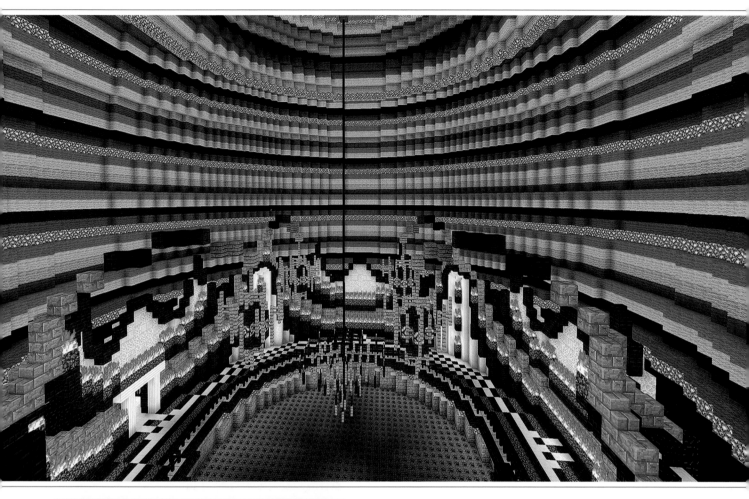

BOW SPLEEF ARENA
By: La_Pixel

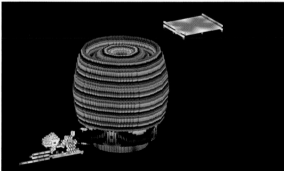

Spleef! Spleef is one of the most common and enduring minigames in Minecraft. For those that haven't had the fun of playing, it basically just involves a flat arena with Wool blocks for a floor, and players run around knocking out the blocks trying to get other players to fall. Bow Spleef uses, as you might guess, Bows to do that, and is one of the more popular variants of Minecraft's favorite little game. This is an arena in which to get your Bow Spleefin' on, and its multicolored striped sphere look is eye-catching and inspired. It also includes everything you need to Spleef right, like observation posts and an entrance way (most Spleef games are teleported to from servers, so they need somewhere to enter), and it would work great on just about any server.

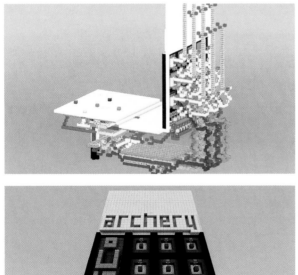

DISCO ARCHERY
By: Disco

Disco makes many appearances in this book, and if you look at these builds you can see why. Disco builds, like those of FillzMinecraft, are instantly recognizable as such, and they're also heavily inventive on the fun end of things. This particular build is kind of like a carnival shooter game, where stuff pops up and you try your best to snipe it before it ducks away. Since this is Minecraft, you'll need your trusty Bow and some serious shootin' skills to do well in Disco's archery minigame, which will keep track of your score, reset itself automatically, and has three levels of difficulty to try out.

CONNECT FOUR
By: FillzMinecraft

It's interesting, but for some Minecraft Redstone creators, you can actually recognize their builds just by looking at it. For those just starting with Redstone, getting something to work at all is good enough and how it looks barely matters, but when crafters get really good at it, they start to develop a distinctive look to their builds that's all their own. Thus is the case for FillzMinecraft, a creator who is great at minigames and who has a highly recognizable style. Part of that is the colors he uses, and part is the way he lays out their Redstone, in this case as a column behind the build not visible as you play. And yes, the game does work!

Screenshot: Minecraft® ™ & © 2009–2015 Mojang/Notch.

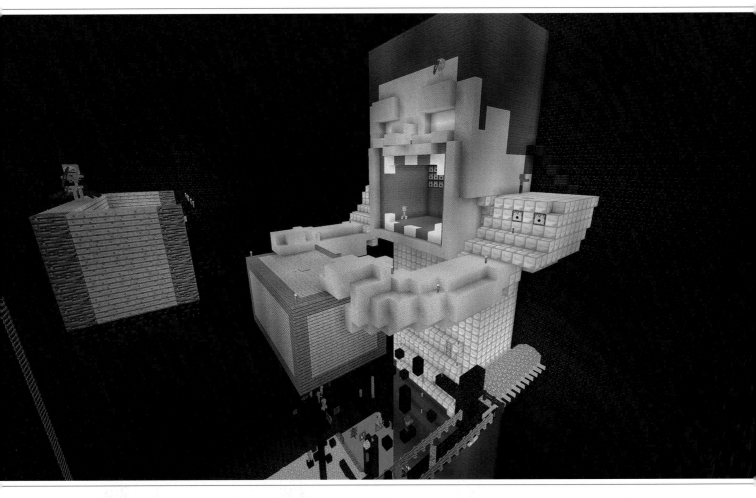

HEROBRINE BOSS
By: SpeedyCrafting

"Boss battles" are a type of minigame that basically involve having a big crafted character as the central figure for a series of challenges, usually made up of waves of mobs. SpeedyCrafting and his crew are known for creating such battles, and this is one that they've said is much harder than some of their earlier creations. From the Planet Minecraft entry, here's what you'll be facing if you dare to challenge the dark and dangerous Herobrine (Minecraft's biggest legend):

Wave 1: [Easy] Parkour & hit all of the redstone lamps. The door to Wave 2 will open when you've hit the 4 redstone lamps.

Wave 2: [Hard!] Parkour & flip the right levers. The levers are on Herobrine's body. The door to Wave 3 will open when you've hit the 3 right levers.

Wave 3: [Hard Too!] Wave 3 is a 1 vs. 1, face to face battle with Herobrine. Like in the picture, you have to climb into his head and smash 23 mobs into his neck (the creeper-face hole). Press the pressure plate on the wooden "chest" to spawn the mobs. After you've smashed the 23 mobs in it, Herobrine will explode, and his eyes will stop glowing.

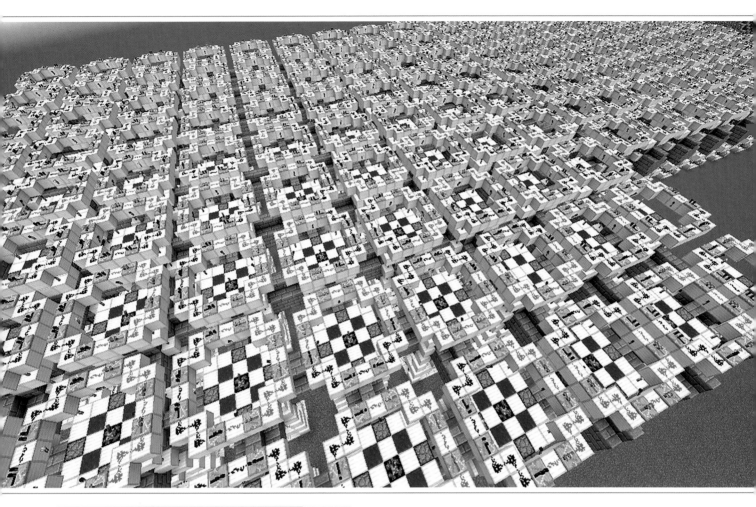

LE LABYRINTHE DE ZEPHIRR
By: MinecraftZephirr

Mazes are something you see a lot of in Minecraft builds, as is Redstone, but a Redstone maze that builds itself as you go completely randomly? There aren't many of those, and Le Labyrinthe de Zephirr may be one of the most fascinating ones yet created. From above it is a gorgeous repetitive array of rooms and Redstone, making for some of the prettiest pictures (we think) that we've taken in Minecraft, but inside it's quite different. When you enter, you can't see out at all and must keep going from room to room, but as you go, the entrances to the rooms will close up and open to create new patterns and to change the maze right before your eyes. It's VERY confusing, but also thoroughly awesome, and it is one of our very favorite builds.

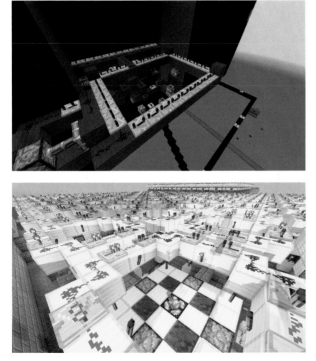

MINECRAFT GAME SHOW
By: Nboss233

Fans of the TV show *Wipeout* will recognize this instantly, and guess what? It all works! If you aren't a person who watches wacky TV shows where people have to bounce across obstacle courses, that's basically what happens in *Wipeout*, and Nboss233 has made this one work basically the way the TV show does. It's kind of like parkour maps, in that you mostly are jumping from thing to thing and trying not to fall, and there are a ton of moving parts and crazy obstacles to get through. What's maybe most impressive about it, besides how well they nailed the look of the show, is that there is a giant digital timer on one side that will actually keep track of how fast everyone does it!

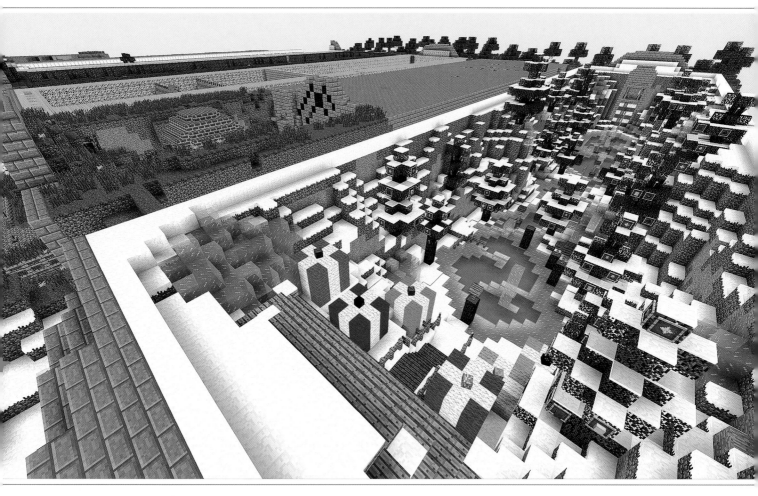

PARKOUR MAP CHRISTMAS CALENDAR
By: minecraft-pg5

One of those groups of builders that is without question among the elite Redstone engineers of the game is minecraft-pg5, and it seems they also know a thing or two about parkour maps from this diabolical array of difficult parkour runs they've built. The "Christmas Calendar" part of this map refers to the fact that there's a different parkour run that you can open up one by one, like those Christmas calendars with the chocolates in them, but you can enjoy this map whenever you wish! Each of the 24 runs (one for each day leading up to the holiday) has its own unique aesthetic and design, and viewing the whole thing from above is very cool, what with all of the various colors and patterns running off in stripes from the center channel. Both impressive visually and a heck of a challenge, this is an example of parkour maps at their best.

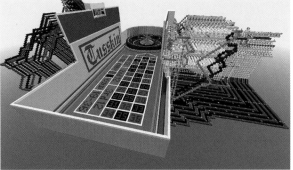

REDSTONE ROULETTE

By: Tusskin

This recreation of a casino game brings gambling in to Minecraft. Okay, not real gambling- it's actually just a very neat virtual roulette table to play for fun, but it actually does spin (it uses Redstone Lamps that light up to indicate where the "ball" is) and you really can place bets with your friends. Plus, it looks very nice, especially at night when you can really see the glow of the Lamps, and the Redstone it took to make this work is mighty impressive.

RUN STEVE RUN
By: Desdenavo

The "Zombie battle arena" minigame type is another build you'll see a lot, especially on servers, and this is a very nicely designed version of that kind of build. It has the standard arena, where you can set what difficulty of Zombies you face, but it also has a cool feature that lets you trade in the items dropped by killed Zombies to get weapons and armor. The idea is to try and last 'til wave nine, at which point Desdenavo says that "special Zombies will spawn."

SLIDE PUZZLE
By: FillzMinecraft

Another awesome Fillz build (can you tell he likes numbers and minigames yet?), this one involves the player trying to slide a grid of numbers around until they are in order from 1-14. It's much harder than it looks, as you can only slide a number to the one empty spot, and Fillz has challenged the internet to see who can be the one to do it in the fewest moves. When you get it right, the game will announce it to you with a special song! It's pretty impressive for the Redstone here to be able to display and move numbers about, remembering where they are and knowing where they should be for a win, and if you peek around at the Redstone (which features Fillz's signature colored blocks as supports), you can tell the amount of hard work it took to make this function.

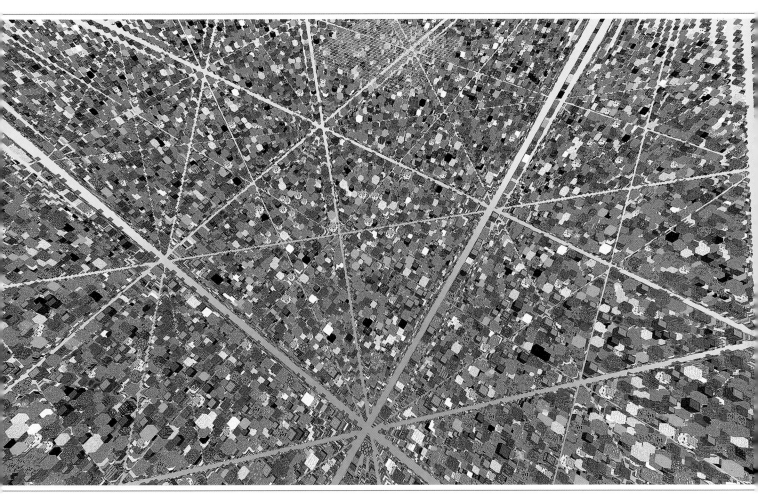

SKYGRID SURVIVAL MAP
By: SethBling

Skyblock is a highly popular minigame type that involves players having to survive and build things (often to complete challenges) in maps that have almost nothing but very small blocks of land floating in the sky. SkyGrid, on the other hand, is a lot crazier. Created by another Minecraft hero and Redstone genius, the SkyGrid is a seemingly never-ending series of single blocks of all kinds in a massive floating grid structure. Survival is still key, and you have to jump from block to block collecting what you can and trying not to fall, eventually building yourself a little floating haven among the many blocks. With the insane number of blocks and the crazy looks of this confusing but awesome map, every play of SkyGrid is going to be completely unique and a lot of fun.

SUPER PIG POWERED SLOT MACHINE
By: Disco

You really just can't have a book of awesome Minecraft builds without a lot of Disco creations in it, because almost nobody makes builds that look this unique. Case in point- the SUPER Pig Powered Slot Machine, which is pretty much what it sounds like. It's not just that the Pigs make up the look of this thing, it actually does run by using Pigs (and a lot of Redstone), and it works just like a real-life slot machine, though it takes Diamonds instead of coins. So slap some Diamonds in there, pull the lever, and see what you win!

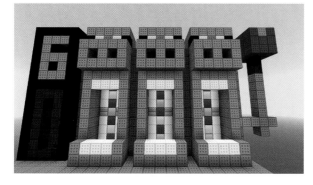

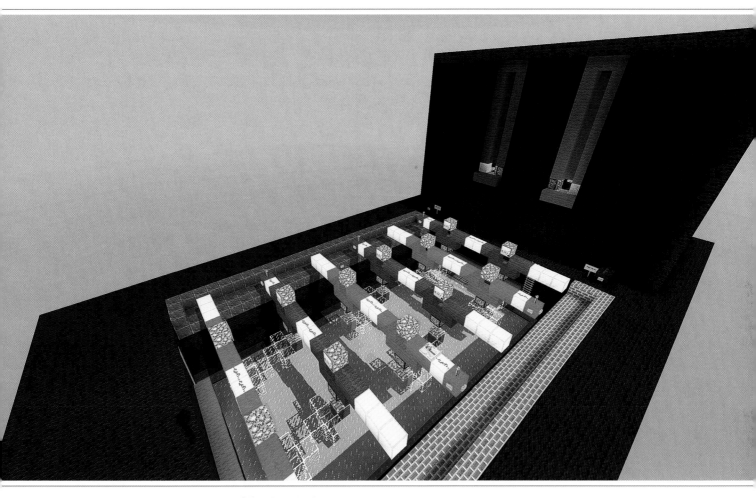

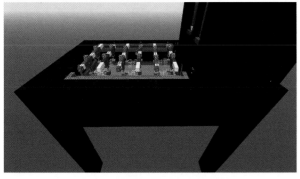

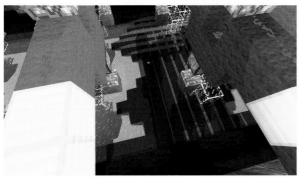

WORKING FOOSBALL TABLE
By: SethBling

SethBling is king when Redstone's the thing, and one of his more fun and competitive builds is this inventive foosball table. It is quite big and looks very much like a real table, and it uses Water that is activated around a player's "men" when the button corresponding with that man is pressed to shove a "ball" around (an item that is pushed by the Water). It's not exactly as fast-paced as traditional foosball, but it does make for a good fun competition with a friend, as the running around and picking which player to use can get difficult and strategic (as well as a bit chaotic). The game will even keep score for you, and it resets itself automatically!

Natural

HUB TERRAFORM
By: Gigorahk

Hub Terraform is a build quite defined by its name. On one hand, it's a hub, which can either refer to general circular structures where things join together, or in Minecraft terms refers to a type of place in Minecraft which servers use as a central location between various parts of the server. People often create maps for servers to use like this, and the maps often can't be escaped except by portals that the users set up on the build themselves. On the other hand, this natural build is a terraform because it is one that involved Gigorahk, the creator, terraforming, which means manipulating earth and plant and water to create a new thing. It's also a "terra" (earth) "form," which could be a noun that refers to an earthlike-form. Whichever way you take the name (and note, it's not all that common to use "terraform" this way in Minecraft, though we like it!), it's a beautiful build, especially from surface level.

THE TREE OF KAJIN
By: Techno

There is some unnatural stuff in this build, such as the village below the towering Tree of Kajin, but the tree itself represents a high-quality entry in one of the genres of Minecraft natural builds, which is of course the genre of giant freakin' trees. Trees are a compelling subject, and Minecraft's standard blocksets lend themselves readily to the creation of these most earth-representative of plants. Just as they so often make them the subjects of paintings and other art, people have gone nuts over recreating trees in Minecraft on a large scale, and Kajin is one of the best available. A tremendous jungle tree, Kajin quite obviously dominates the landscape, but it also manages to fit right into it and is deftly crafted to look like something that could easily be natural in a more magical land than native Earth.

MEIVA – DANCE OF THE ELEMENTS
By: Darastlix

Rarely do you see builds that are at once excellent nature builds with a lot of variety and also a concept build, but that's the case with Meiva. Meiva is two islands, one of fire and earth and the other of water and air, and it's shaped in the form of a giant yin-yang symbol, except instead of a circle on each side, there are giant volcanoes. This map is enormous, and each area in it takes up so much space as to look simply like a giant customized biome, and to be quite natural and gorgeous at that. In fact, the whole thing simply feels like two islands, one wintery and one forested with a flaming volcano as its largest feature, each sitting right by the other. The detailing on the biomes created here is incredible, including beautiful frozen sea structures, mountains that heavily outdo vanilla Minecraft mountains in terms of beauty, and a large number of unique structures to discover scattered across the expanses of the two isles.

Redstone

VERTICAL MAN CANNON

By: OliverFrenchie

YES. Launching junk into the air is the BEST, and this 300 block TNT launcher does just that with aplomb. Basically it's just a bit of Redstone rigged up to a small mountain of TNT set up just right, and when you stand on the right spot and flip that ever-lovin' switch, you get yourself a ride straight up into the Minecraft stratosphere on the back of a big dang explosion. This explodey joy is done by being good at the physics of Minecraft and putting the player in the right spot for a perfectly timed explosion, and the result is one of the fastest, highest launches into the rarified air at the top of a Minecraft map that you'll ever see.

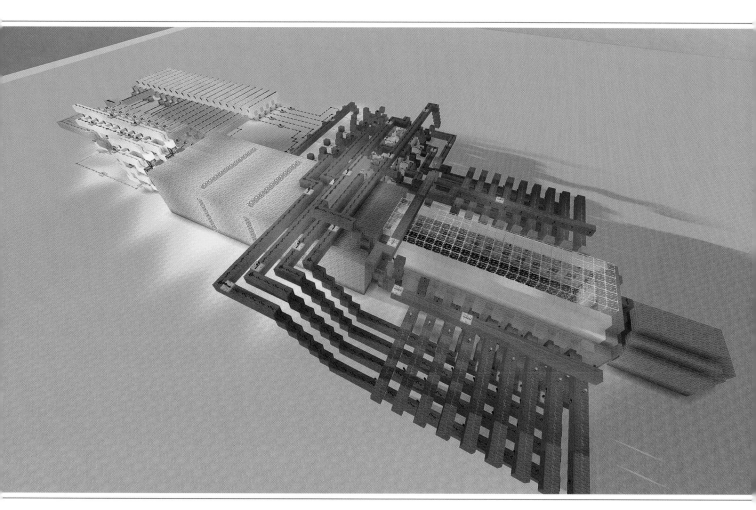

CALCULATOR

By: MDlolxd

This is another representation of a build quite common to Minecraft, this time for the community of Redstone engineers out there. Because of the way Redstone rules work, you can use Redstone signals in the right combinations and patterns to create logic gates, which give you the basic functions needed to build a working calculator (and, as we'll see in a minute, computers!). In the end, the real difficulty with calculators and computers is in designing a Redstone build that actually looks good and is easy to control as much as it is one that actually works. The aesthetics and user experience can in fact be harder to do well than the functions on a basic calculator, because calculators are designed with set rules that don't change, while looks and usability are going to vary greatly from one build to another. This calculator, however, nails all of it neatly, being as fun to look at as it is to use.

FASOLKA III
By:remixis098

You might not know it from looking, but this build is a music studio built within Minecraft! It allows for the creation, storage, editing, and playback of songs using Minecraft's built-in Noteblock system, but making it much more complex by making it all controllable through Redstone. There's a keyboard, sequencers, drum machines, and all of the basics of a very low-level but definitely functional music studio, and it's all done through highly complex, but very well-organized, Redstone wiring.

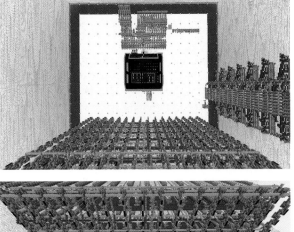

HIDDEN TREE DOOR
By: codecrafted

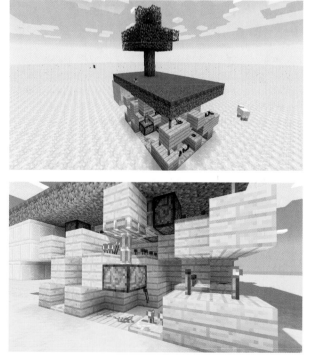

Builder codecrafted is an outright legend in the Minecraft Redstone community, creating some of the game's most memorable Redstone. Typically, codecrafted sticks to medium-sized Redstone builds that are thoroughly efficient and which carry a style aesthetically and functionally that is all code's own, often all in the name of performing a function that is more entertaining and fun than it is really necessary. Stackable melon farms and mass producing sheep farms are among codecrafted's many famous builds, as is this sweet Hidden Tree Door build that requires very little space to give you a very neat entrance to your base or a secret stash. It will move and then replace a Tree all on its own when given the signal, opening a hole through which to enter your building, and it does so in a flush and admirably compact way that few builders can achieve.

LPG'S REDSTONE COMPUTER
By: MasterSwe and Igor_Timofeev

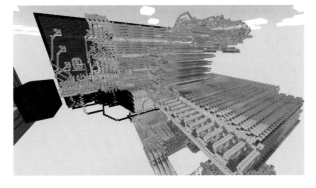

Most veteran Crafters have heard of or seen a computer built with Redstone inside of Minecraft, but it's not often that the builder of that computer actually goes to the extra step of making it look like a computer too. While this machine might not be as powerful as some of the all-function Minecraft computers out there, it more than makes up for it by having a completely working screen and keyboard, acting much like an older regular computer would. Its case, screen, and keyboard setup also look pretty awesome at giant magnitudes, and the Redstone behind the whole thing is a sight to behold.

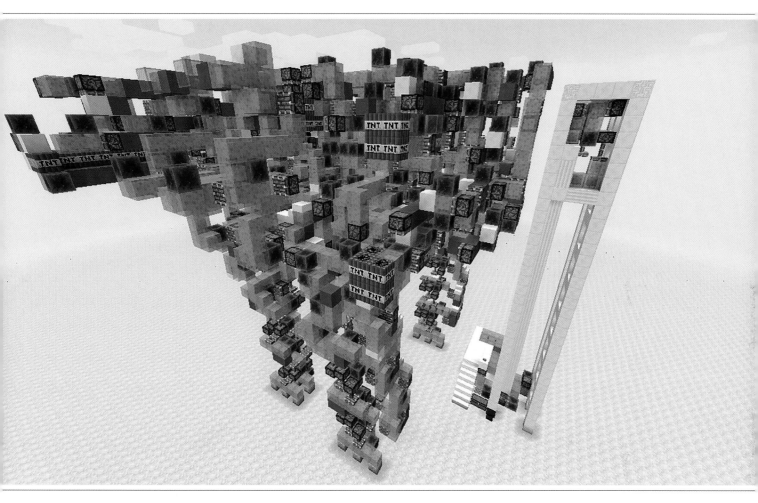

MEGA GARGANTUA
By: Cubehamster

Another build by a true master of Redstone, this time we have a build by the weird genius Cubehamster that's so odd it'd almost be comical if it weren't horrifying in its size and movement. This build is the Mega Gargantua, a shuffling Redstone cannon-laden robot that will start a slow trek across the lands when activated by a player in the driver's spot. As it moves, you can run about lighting the cannons and blowing the crap out of the countryside, moving down area after area as your enormous robo-steed trundles along under its own power. This build is done using the magic of the Slimeblock, whose introduction into Minecraft allowed for the first self-moving vehicles in the game. Cubehamster, a veteran of the Redstone scene and a Redstone magician with a love for complex moving builds, says that he went through over 1,200 versions of this build before getting it right, 90% of which didn't work at all.

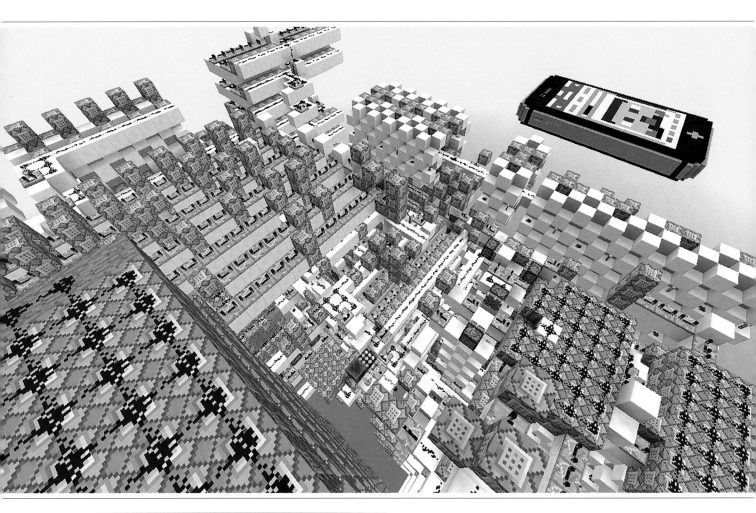

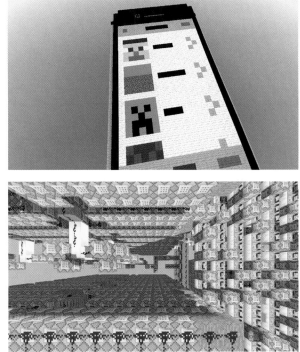

PETER'S WORKING IPHONE
By: Peter-

You read that title right, and seeing this thing in action is even more impressive than it sounds. This gigantic iPhone really does have a touchscreen (made using some proximity sensor trickery), it really does change depending on what options you pick, and it really does have 12 apps to run. This is a build that makes heavy use of the Command Block, a special kind of Redstone block that allows players to essentially write small amounts of code into Minecraft to perform functions that normally could not exist, or which would take an insane amount of Redstone logic gates to make. By getting it just right, Peter- has created something that it's almost hard to believe exists.

PISTON DRIVEN 12HR DIGITAL CLOCK
By: CNBMinecraft

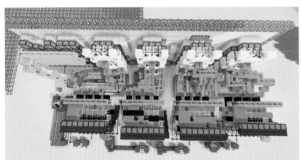

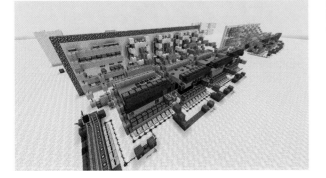

It might seem like a digital clock that uses blocks to physically create its own face and which also keeps time pretty darn well in the game would be hard to make, but the Redstone behind just that build in the case of CNBMinecraft's digital clock is actually quite compact. Because Redstone ticks and transmission are so heavily reliant on timing in the game, clocks that are both totally functioning and which also look beautiful (not to mention that they look quite large, meaning they'd be hard to avoid if put up at the right height and angle) are completely possible without an insane Redstone array. This one is among the top efficient and nice-looking clocks made in the game. You can actually even learn how to make this clock through CNB's awesome tutorials.

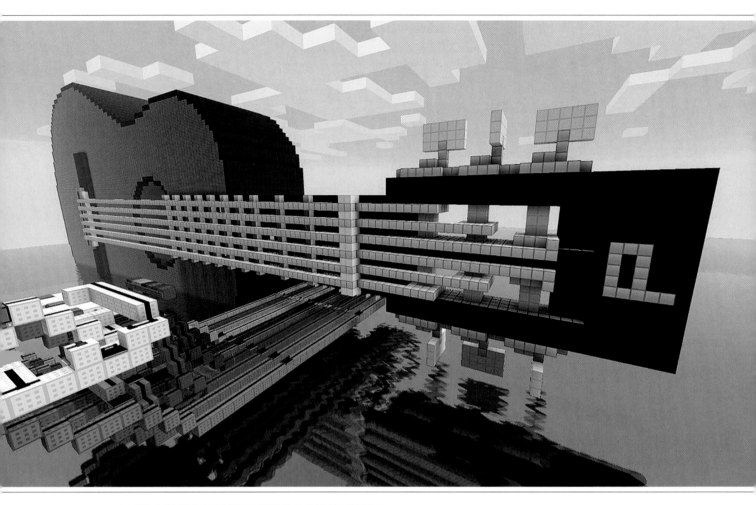

PLAYABLE GUITAR
By: Disco

Even more so than the other geniuses of Redstone listed in this chapter, no name is more respected in the Minecraft wiring universe than that of FVDisco, also known as Disco. Disco has a knack for beautiful, efficient, and brilliant Redstone designs that are immediately recognizable as a Disco build, and which also are incredibly fun to mess around with. In this case, it's a literal playable guitar that Disco has designed for our pleasure. This not only looks exactly like a real guitar (except with Disco's lovely bright, nearly cartoony style), it actually plays in real time and can even do chords and arpeggios. These are controlled with pressure plates and work in loops, and it's just about as much musical fun as you'll ever have in this game.

PROGRAMMABLE DRUM KIT
By: Disco

If you thought the Playable Guitar was great, but you're more of the percussion type, get a load of the Programmable Drum Kit, also by the incredible Disco. This addition to Disco's Minecraft band setup has three different channels with 16 steps each, and different drums on it can be muted and defined as you like. It's even animated! Get your jam on block style, Crafters.

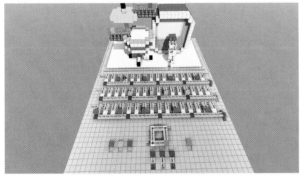

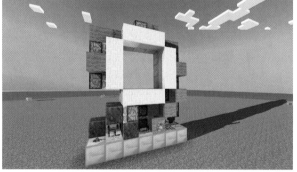

REDSTONE 3X3 AUTOMATIC DOOR
By: MumboJumbo/Your Trusty Author

While the inimitable YouTube Redstone creator and teacher MumboJumbo is the one who made this design popular, you might be interested to know that your very own authors here are the ones who crafted the heck out of this build. Yep! We can do stuff in Minecraft besides just talk about it and take perty pictures too, y'all! This build is actually a great one to learn when in the process of becoming a Redstone engineer yourself, as it is both awesome to see work and it teaches some essential and advanced Redstone concepts like falling edges. Typical, basic (i.e. not awesome enough) Redstone doors are limited to being 2 blocks wide or tall, as the middle blocks aren't easily moved by Pistons (the typical way to make doors), but through using said advanced techniques and some efficiency smarts, this door does the deed and doesn't take much space at all while doing it.

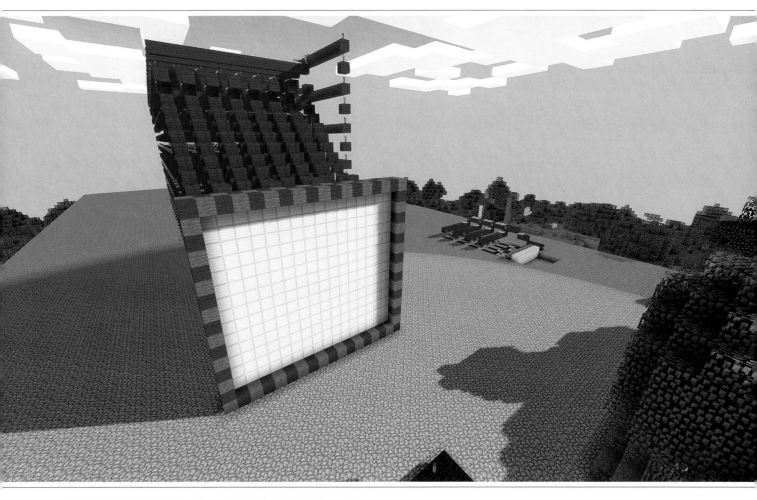

TV PROJECT
By: seabiskut227

It's a common Redstone dream to perform animation and/or screen-like functions by using the items and blocks already available in Minecraft, and this is one such creation. It essentially makes a screen out of blocks into a programmable grid that will change its look based on whatever input you create. Over a set amount of time it will cycle through your changes, creating basic images at your command. It's not exactly *Phineas and Ferb,* but we think for a TV created inside of a video game that was never meant to do anything of the sort, it's downright amazing.

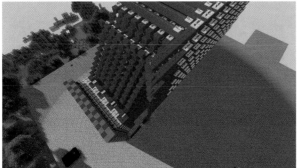

Unique Builds

AWESOME MINECRAFT HUB
By: TheRoyalPixels

Here's another gorgeous hub to use on server worlds, this time with built-in signs and hallways. These are made to be easily configured with the server's own minigames or server sections, so players can see where different things are in the server from afar and head right to them. The hub has a lot of lovely natural elements to it, including some surrounding mammoth trees, as well as a fantasy temple vibe going on. It even looks great at night!

CAVE SETTLEMENT
By: JelleB14

It doesn't get much more unique than Cave Settlement when it comes to breaking up the rules of building! JelleB14 made this inventive cave and mountain combo when he was tired of doing big builds and wanted to stretch his capabilities. What resulted is a very cool build that goes all the way to the sky and has features like a dock, a water-filled cave, an underground hangout, two marketplaces, and a giant mansion on top! There's a path running through this whole thing that goes from the bottom to the top, and it's really a nice little walk. It just shows you that putting some limits on a build can help you be more creative in ways you wouldn't have previously thought.

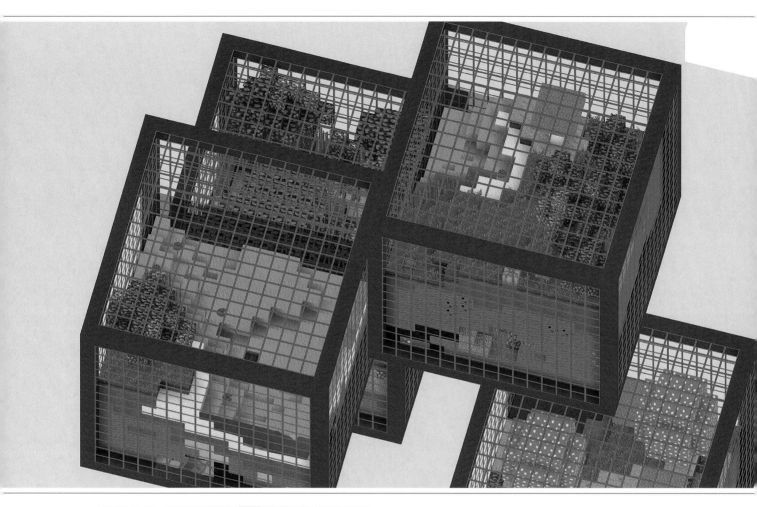

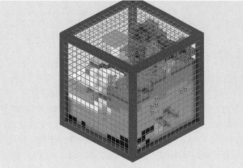

CUBE SURVIVAL
By: Nefashus

Survival in Minecraft is a bit tricky at first, but by the time you get some tools and food sources goin', it becomes pretty easy. Dying is not much of a big problem at that point, and you do it rarely even then. If you're looking for more of a challenge when it comes to making it to the next day in Minecraft, perhaps if you're a fan of other survival games like The Long Dark, Cube Survival is a map set that makes it much more of a difficult task to keep on keepin' on. It massively limits what you have available to you as a player, forcing you to use everything at your disposal efficiently and carefully to craft what you need to keep surviving, and if you mess up, well, you'll just have to start over. It's a very fun way to spice up regular Minecraft play, and it will show you just how good your skills are in this little game.

DIRT HOUSE

By: Valorman1, SCritescu, MrHappyTinkles, Sentaul, Sentaru, Carlotta4th, Trammerse, Jamriko, Juno, Xorama, Aninochi, Jared4242, LadyFajra, Jfontain, Jakar_Windsailor, Nil8, Ezzick, Onyx_Reaper

Apparently on some Minecraft servers "I built a dirt house today" is an uncommon thing to hear, perhaps because it's funny and very few people do it. Inspired by that comment, the group of builders listed above from the Valorian Minecraft Server took on the task to make a Dirt house look good, and boy did they! The result of their efforts was a gorgeous, delicately balanced mansion with so many rooms that the creators get lost in it and say they don't even know how big it is. It has a sweeping grand main hallway with a pool, gardens, helicopter pads, a fleet of giant chickens out back (what?), a theater, a library, and oh so much more. Well done, builders!

ETERNAL'S HAVEN
By: Murps

Eternal's Haven is a city with a bit of fantasy and a bit of sci-fi, but we put it here in the unique chapter because WOW, just look at this thing! This is one we highly recommend downloading and exploring, because the level of creativity is outright off the charts. Just from our last trip through, we saw a dude riding on the back of a giant eagle, one of the most decked-out marketplaces in Minecraft, and a freaking massive steam-powered dragon with an entire world on its wings! The Victorian style of the floating buildings in this build is inspired by *Bioshock Infinite*, but everything else in it is just straight up genius imagination pouring out of Murps' mind, and that one person did this build alone is mind-boggling.

FROSTY THE SNOWMAN
By: _themineman23_

Talk about chilling; this enormous angry snowman is nightmare fodder if there ever was any inside of this game. Ole frosty here only took a few hours to complete, and yet the style on this big, bad boy is out of this world. Getting something to look organic and almost alive is pretty tough in MC, especially at enormous sizes like this, and the builders here just nailed it. The use of lava for a scarf and the glowing eyes is a stroke of genius, and it also serves to make this thing just as frightening at night (maybe more so!). Well done!

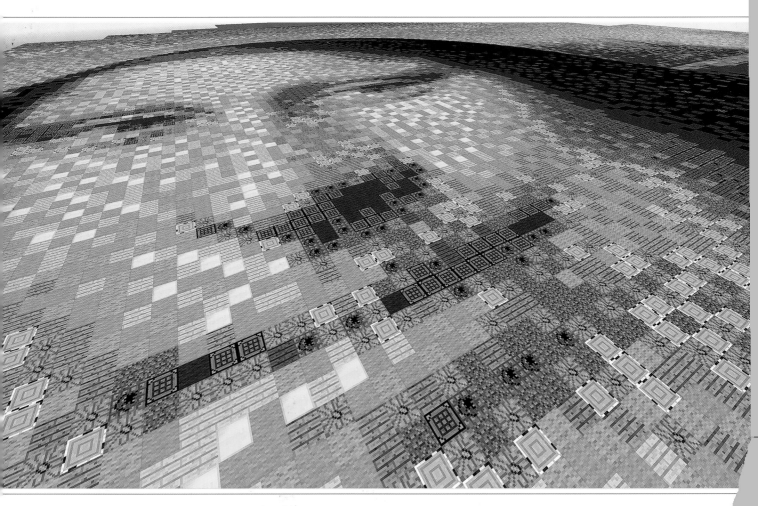

MONA LISA
By: CrystalBlocks

There's pixel art in Minecraft (using blocks as individual pixels in an image), and then there's this *Mona Lisa* by CrystalBlocks. Having been Crafters for a long time, and having done just about every type of building there is, we still don't know how CrystalBlocks managed to get this build so exact. There's even shading, and the background looks quite like it does in the real painting! The eyes and the mouth are dead on! HOW?! It's incredible, and getting up close to it makes it even more so, as you can see that the creators used not only Wool blocks of solid color, but also many other types of blocks to achieve the high quality of this masterpiece.